P9-DIA-614

# Stations of the Nativity

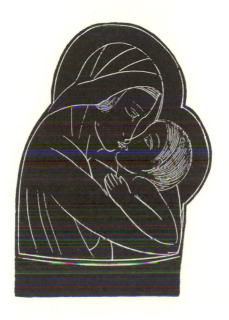

Copyright ©1999 Raymond Chapman

Originally published in English under the title *Stations of the Nativity* by the Canterbury Press Norwich of St. Mary's Works, St. Mary's Plain, Norwich, Norfolk NR3 3BH UK

**Morehouse Publishing**
P.O. Box 1321
Harrisburg, PA 17105

*Morehouse Publishing is a division of The Morehouse Group.*

All rights reserved. No part of this book may be reproduced or transmitted in any form or by any means, electronic or mechanical, including photocopying, recording, or by any information storage and retrieval system, without written permission from the publisher.

The Author asserts the moral right to be identified as the Author of this work.

*Printed in the United States of America*

*Cover design by Corey Kent*

*A Catalog record for this book is available from the Library of Congress.*

ISBN 0-8192-1804-9

# Stations *of* *the* Nativity

*Meditations on the*
*Incarnation of Christ*

Raymond Chapman

with illustrations selected by
Dame Winefride Pruden

MOREHOUSE PUBLISHING

Also from the same author
and available from Morehouse Publishing


*The Habit of Prayer—a round-the-year prayer guide*
and
*Stations of the Resurrection*

# Contents

# Suggestions for Using this Book

The Way of the Cross is a traditional exercise of devotion, in which we follow with awe and penitence the steps of Jesus to Calvary and the tomb. In a previous book, *Stations of the Resurrection*, I have offered a similar series of prayers and meditations on the Resurrection appearances of our Lord. The redemptive suffering of the Cross and the glory of the Resurrection were made possible by the coming of the Son of God into this world, to take our human nature upon himself. It is in Bethlehem that the story of our salvation begins.

The events preceding and following the Nativity are here set out in fourteen stations. The meditations and prayers accompanying each of them may be used for either personal or corporate devotion, as the Stations of the Cross are used by many worshippers. In a conducted progress around a church, in gathered prayer or in private

reflection, the devotion may be particularly suitable for the forty days from Christmas to the Feast
of the Presentation, but it is appropriate for any
time in the year because the grace of the
Incarnation is always among us.

Each of the stations has the relevant biblical
passage, a short consideration, and prayers of
thanksgiving and penitence with versicles and
responses to introduce and link each station.
Pictures are added which may aid devotion.
Suggested prayers and hymns for beginning and
ending the whole devotion may be appropriate
when it is led by a conductor.

All the stations here set out are based on Gospel
accounts. It is not necessary to try to harmonize
them into a continuous narrative; each reveals
some truth of the experience of the witnesses, and
of ourselves.

For more extended use of the stations, each
has a longer meditation focusing more fully on
what that particular event in the early life of
Jesus may be saying to us and more intimately
relating it to the recorded story. These meditations are probably most suitable for individual
devotion with one or a few stations at a time. It
is suggested that those following this method
should first reflect more deeply on the Gospel
reading. You may wish to follow the shorter
devotions of the station as a preparation for

meditation and resolution. Each meditation ends with a short petition, to carry the fruit of devotion into the life of the day.

# Introduction

Christmas is certainly the most popular festival of the Christian year. For many people it begins with preparations over a month before, is celebrated with cards, presents, parties and special meals, and is considered to be over within a few days. It attracts more people to at least one church service than any other time, with congregations almost everywhere outnumbering those of Easter.

Christians are by no means required to stand apart from the more secular pleasures of a break in the middle of winter and the many things that are good in shared rejoicing. This is part of God's gift to us in the world of his bountiful creation. But it is too easy to keep Christmas both in pleasure and in worship, and not to be fully mindful of the Nativity which gives it meaning. We are not likely to forget the events of the first Easter; every Sunday is a special observance of the Resurrection, and daily recognition of the presence of the risen Christ both confirms and strengthens our faith. Christmas, partly because of the long work of preparation – which often obscures the true preparation of Advent – seems to come and go and be forgotten for the rest of the year.

The Christmas season can well be seen as extending to the Presentation of Christ in the Temple on 2 February. This gives a period of forty days, a parallel to the duration of Lent and Easter, in which to celebrate the Incarnation and give proper regard to the Epiphany themes. Easter must always be at the heart of the Christian faith, leading from the Cross to the assurance of new life. But there would have been no Cross and no Resurrection without the Nativity. The Christian faith is a faith of incarnation, of the mystery whereby God the Son, the second Person of the Holy Trinity, became fully human for the sake of the whole human race. As the Christmas collect says, he came to 'take our nature upon him and as at this time to be born of a pure virgin.' Our Christmas hymns, sung repeatedly in December and scarcely ever heard for the rest of the year, remind us of the result of the Incarnation. 'God and sinners reconciled' – 'Born that Man no more may die' – God's wondrous love in saving lost mankind' – 'To save us all from Satan's power' – 'To be our Redeemer from death, hell and sin'.

The early Fathers of the Church gave great

weight to the Incarnation. They found in it a double consequence, that the act of divinity in assuming humanity unites us in a new way with God, whose perfection we can never approach by ourselves. 'He took our flesh, to the end that he might show that the law of the flesh had been subjected to the law of the mind' (St Ambrose). 'Having become what we were, he through himself again united humanity to God' (St Gregory of Nyssa). 'He became Son of Man, who was God's own Son, in order that he might make the children of men to be children of God' (St John Chrysostom). 'He was made man that we might be made God; and he manifested himself by a body that we might receive the idea of the unseen Father' (St Athanasius).

The stories of the birth of Jesus come to us through the Gospels of St Matthew and St Luke. There are differences of detail and it is not possible to harmonize them completely, but they agree on the divine announcement of God's plan, conception by the Holy Spirit and birth at Bethlehem by the Virgin Mary. Luke tells the story through the experience of Mary, which he may well have heard from her own lips. He records her being with the disciples after the Ascension (Acts 1:14). The legend that he painted a portrait of her is probably not true, but it shows that of all the Evangelists, he was particularly associated with her. Matthew sees some of the events through Joseph. As throughout his Gospel, he emphasizes the links with traditional Judaism, but it is he also who records the Magi, the first Gentiles to see the infant Christ. St John has no nativity story, but he gives us a deep reflection on the theology of the Incarnation by which 'the Word was made flesh and dwelt among us.'

St Paul has much to say of the wonderful act of incarnation by which the Son of God 'emptied himself, taking the form of a slave, being born in human likeness' (Philippians 2:6). 'God sent his Son, born of a woman, born under the law' (Galatians 4:4). For him, the reconciliation between God and sinful humanity makes Christ the Second Adam, restoring through human nature what had been lost by the Fall and all subsequent sin (1 Corinthians 15: 45–9).

The Nativity is the birth of one and the new birth of many, through all the generations of believers that were to come. The events from Good Friday to Easter Day would complete the transformation, but this is where it all began.

Let us then keep Christmas with every sort of rejoicing, but let us honour the Nativity at other times as well. The forty days to the Presentation give us much material for devotion and medita-tion. During the long summer Trinity season, we can hold together the wonder of both Christmas

and Easter, drawing continually on the insights
which we have gained at the time of their special
observances. Easter lifts us to the things eternal:
Christmas affirms this world as God's creation,
loved by him in spite of sin, made new by his own
gracious act. The two worlds are drawn together,
so that whenever we enjoy human pleasures we
can offer them also in the light of eternity.

# Before the Stations

*Almighty God, whose blessed Son took our human nature so that we might regain our lost innocence and be restored to the divine image that was disfigured by sin, grant that as we meditate on the mystery of his humanity we may share the glory of his divinity, who lives and reigns in the unity of the Holy Trinity, Father, Son and Holy Spirit, now and for ever. Amen.*

A hymn may be sung: the familiar Christmas hymns tell of the wonder of the Incarnation and the following are particularly suitable:

A great and mighty wonder

Hark, the herald angels sing

In the bleak midwinter

Of the Father's heart begotten

The great God of heaven is come down to earth

# 1

# Zechariah

V We adore thee O Christ and we bless thee.
R Because by thy wonderful Nativity thou hast
given us new birth.

*In the days of King Herod of Judaea, there was a
priest named Zechariah. Once when he was serving as priest before God, there appeared to him an
angel of the Lord. The angel said to him, 'Do not be
afraid, Zechariah, for your prayer has been heard.
Your wife Elizabeth will bear a son, and you will
name him John. He will turn many of the people of
Israel to the Lord their God.' Zechariah said to the
angel, 'How will I know that this is so? For I am an
old man, and my wife is getting on in years.' The
angel replied, 'Because you did not believe my
words, you will become mute, unable to speak,
until the days these things occur.'*

(Luke 1: part of verses 3–20)

Zechariah was serving the worship in the Temple
as it had been done for centuries past. In those
years many prophets had declared God's purpose

for his people and told of the Messiah who was to come. Now the time was near, and Zechariah would have a son who would be the last prophet of the Old Covenant and the forerunner of the New. It was too much for the old man to believe. He was deprived of speech and sent to meditate in silence until the promise was fulfilled.

We give thanks to God for his patience, the constancy of his love, the assurance of his promises. We give thanks for the teaching of his prophets, for all his words of preparation which were fulfilled in the gospel. We give thanks for his gifts which continually exceed our expectations.

We too are slow to believe, because the good news seems impossible in human terms. We lose hope too readily, grow weary of waiting and turn aside from the way that we should follow. Teach us always to know that your ways are not our ways and that nothing will prevent the fulfilment of your living purpose.

V   God sent his Son into the world.
R   To bring us to eternal life.
V   Let us bless the Lord.
R   Thanks be to God.

✠

The time of waiting is time wasted as we count
time in this world.

We fret as we wait for the bus, for the
examination result, for the surgery bell,
and resent the time we could, as we think, use
more to our advantage.

God's time of waiting is different; it is patient,
creative, purposeful.

It is the love of a father who knows when it is
time to give and when to withhold.

It is the compassion that reveals itself when we
are ready and open to receive it.

Centuries of our time passed until time and place
were ready together.

Time passed in Jerusalem, the holy city, the
chosen place,
where the sacrifices were offered and the
covenant kept,
where the prophets were stoned and the
covenant broken.

But always the patience of love, waiting itself to
follow the way of suffering.

Waiting with God is not time lost but time of
    being truly alive.
Speech is silent as the wonder is revealed.

*Patient God, turn my anxiety and anger into
    patience.*

*Unchanging God, turn my restlessness into quiet
    and constancy.*

*Faithful God, turn my doubts and fears into
    assurance.*

*Please, show me when to speak and when to listen.*

# 2

# Annunciation

V   We adore thee O Christ and we bless thee.
R   **Because by thy wonderful Nativity thou hast given us new birth.**

*The angel Gabriel was sent by God to a town in Galilee called Nazareth, to a virgin engaged to a man whose name was Joseph, of the house of David. The angel said to her, 'Do not be afraid, Mary, for you have found favour with God. And now, you will conceive in your womb and bear a son, and you will name him Jesus. He will be great, and will be called the Son of the Most High.' Mary said to the angel, 'How can this be, since I am a virgin?' The angel said to her, 'The Holy Spirit will come upon you, and the power of the Most High will overshadow you; therefore, the child to be born will be holy; he will be called Son of God.' Then Mary said, 'Here am I, the servant of the Lord; let it be with me according to your word.'*

(Luke 2: part of verses 26–37)

In the Old Testament narratives angels are sent to

make known a great work that God is about to perform. The births of Isaac and of Samson are announced in this way. Now the angel Gabriel comes to a young woman in a small town to tell her of the most wonderful birth in all history. After her first alarm and incredulity, she calmly believes and accepts the will of God.

We give thanks for the example of the Blessed Virgin Mary, our pattern of purity, humility and absolute trust. As she knew by the message of an angel that she would be the mother of the Incarnate Son of God, give us grace to hear your word and follow your call, whether it be to little or great work in your service.

We do not trust in what the power of God can do with our weakness. We think that we can find our own way, instead of seeking to follow where you are leading. Forgive our slowness of mind and hardness of heart, and make us your servants according to your word in our own time and place.

V   God sent his Son into the world.
R   To bring us to eternal life.
V   Let us bless the Lord.
R   Thanks be to God.

✠

On an ordinary spring day, she did not expect
    anything to happen because she was one of
    the quiet people who ask for little.

Lords of a higher creation did not pass that way
until an angel, shafted in new season sunlight,
spoke to her with the heavenly salutation of her
    Maker,
Father of all sending the uncreated, the only-
    begotten,
to be the newly-begotten, the weak and
    vulnerable.

The power of the Spirit, unseen, overshadowing,
the still small voice more powerful than thunder,
breathed life into the womb of innocence,
Son of the Highest, son of a virgin.

She bowed beneath the Word's weight told
and graciously accepted uncovenanted grace.

When we are too busy to notice them,
angels may pass through the familiar room
sometimes with human voices, sometimes in
    silent love.
calling, promising, pointing the way –
because things happen when God wills them
and not when we think it is appropriate.

✠

*When the will is rebellious, may I know the
   obedience of Mary.*

*When pride builds a wall around me, may I know
   the humility of Mary.*

*When the flesh is weak and clamorous, may I
   know the purity of Mary.*

# 3

# Visitation

V   We adore thee O Christ and we bless thee.
R   Because by thy wonderful Nativity thou hast
given us new birth.

*In those days Mary set out and went with haste to
a Judaean town in the hill country where she
entered the house of Zechariah and greeted
Elizabeth. When Elizabeth heard Mary's greeting,
the child leapt in her womb. And Elizabeth was
filled with the Holy Spirit and exclaimed with a
loud cry, 'Blessed are you among women, and
blessed is the fruit of your womb. And why has this
happened to me, that the mother of my Lord comes
to me? For as soon as I heard the sound of your
greeting, the child in my womb leapt for joy. And
blessed is she who believed that there would be a
fulfilment of what was spoken to her by the Lord.'
And Mary said,*

> *'My soul magnifies the Lord,
> and my spirit rejoices in God my Saviour.'*

(Luke 1: 39–47)

Visitation

We read of a movingly natural and human response to the message of the angel. Mary goes to tell the strange story to her cousin Elizabeth, who is already expecting a child. As the two women greet each other, the presence of the divine brings a response from Elizabeth's unborn son: the Baptist, still in the womb, already acknowledges the coming of One much greater than himself. Mary, no longer fearful, breaks into a song of joy and praise.

**We give thanks for the mutual support of family and friends, for their love and sympathy in the great moments of life. Give us grace to value human love more deeply, to show it in our concern for others and to see in it a shadow of the divine love.**

**We fail to recognize the presence of holiness in our daily lives. We do not reverence life itself as a miracle of God's bounty. Help us to acknowledge the divine spirit in other people and to honour them because they are created in love.**

V    God sent his Son into the world.
R    To bring us to eternal life.
V    Let us bless the Lord.
R    Thanks be to God.

✠

Did the sun shine, there among the hills,
casting light on the young girl filled with such
    amazing news?

Now that angels were gentle as well as powerful,
there was no fear, only awe and wonder
and the need to confide in that kind, wise
    woman,
nearer in blood, older in generation.

They embraced, Mary whispering her secret,
and Elizabeth felt the strange stirring – not the
    usual movement
but a joy that ran through all her being
that her child was sharing the time of growth
    with his Maker,
and that this girl, known and loved from her own
    childhood,
was to be the Mother of the Lord.

As Mary went away, the hills kept the secret for a
    season,
that two women had shared woman's greatest joy
and the whole world was coming again to birth.

✠

*Saviour God, let me rejoice in you:*

*I rejoice in the holiness of your Name,*
*I rejoice in your mercy to those who acknowledge*
    *you,*
*I rejoice in your love for the humble and meek,*
*I rejoice in the bounty of your spiritual food,*
*I rejoice in the assurance of your promises.*

*But when I fail to rejoice with all my heart*
*Please, do not send me empty away.*

# 4

# Birth of the Baptist

V   We adore thee O Christ and we bless thee.
R   Because by thy wonderful Nativity thou hast given us new birth.

*Now the time came for Elizabeth to give birth, and she bore a son. On the eighth day they came to circumcise the child, and they were going to name him Zechariah after his father. But his mother said, 'No; he is to be called John.' Then they began motioning to his father to find out what name he wanted to give him. He asked for a writing-tablet and wrote, 'His name is John.' And immediately his mouth was opened and his tongue freed, and he began to speak, praising God. Fear came over all their neighbours, and all these things were talked about throughout the entire hill country of Judaea. All who heard them pondered them and said, 'What will this child become?' For, indeed, the hand of the Lord was with him.*

(Luke 2: part of verses 57–66)

The first son would be likely to take his father's name, or one already known in the family. John's

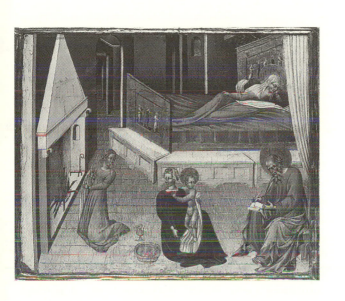

parents obeyed the command of the angel and gave him a name which in its Hebrew form means 'God has been gracious'. This child was to be the forerunner of God's most gracious gift to the human race. As soon as the name was given, Zechariah spoke again in the words of the Benedictus:

'Blessed be the Lord God of Israel,
    for he has visited and redeemed his people
And has raised up a mighty salvation for us
    in the house of his servant David.'

**We give thanks for the revelation of God's will in what may seem unimportant. We praise him for his loving preparation for the coming of his Son, until the day when John would declare the good news of salvation. We pray for grace to discern when our lives are being prepared for new service.**

**We do not trust in the fulfilment of the divine promises. We take the easy, familiar decision, thinking that we know what is best. Help us to listen more earnestly for God's word to us and to follow it more faithfully.**

V    God sent his Son into the world.
R    **To bring us to eternal life.**
V    Let us bless the Lord.
R    **Thanks be to God.**

✠

It seemed there would be no greater wonder
than a son of their old age, named by divine
     decree.

Prophecy became reality, the dumb spoke,
the power of God came among his people,
the true light was coming into the world
and the best was still to be revealed.

The witness-bearer, now weak and speechless,
first token of redeeming love,
was waiting for the time to be fulfilled,
wilderness years, healing water, the new land of
     promise.

His work accomplished, the good news
     proclaimed,
he would decrease and pass into the shadows,
rejoicing, as the sword fell,
that God's ancestral promises would be faithful for
     ever.

*Lord, deliver me from evil and let me serve you
     without fear,
Lord, deliver me from the shadow of sin and give
     light in my darkness,
Lord, deliver me from error and guide me into the
     way of peace.*

# 5

# Joseph's Dream

V   We adore thee O Christ and we bless thee.
R   Because by thy wonderful Nativity thou hast
     given us new birth.

*When his mother Mary had been engaged to
Joseph, but before they lived together, she was
found to be with child by the Holy Spirit. Her husband Joseph, being a righteous man and unwilling
to expose her to public disgrace, planned to dismiss
her quietly. But just when he had resolved to do
this, an angel of the Lord appeared to him in a
dream and said, 'Joseph, son of David, do not be
afraid to take Mary as your wife, for the child conceived in her is from the Holy Spirit. She will bear
a son, and you are to name him Jesus, for he will
save his people from their sins.' When Joseph awoke
from sleep, he did as the Lord commanded him.*
                        (Matthew 2: part of verses 18–24)

The story tells of what seemed to be an event of
disappointment and sorrow. Joseph was distressed
beyond measure, torn between his own grief and

his desire not to harm the woman he loved. Again, God revealed the wonderful identity of Mary's child and, like her, Joseph believed and was faithful. He accepted his destiny to nurture and protect the son that was not his own but was entrusted to his fatherly care.

We give thanks for the gift of those who are close to us and whom we trust; for the love which endures through doubts and difficulties. Give us hearts more grateful for the human love that is a continual image of the divine love, ever seeking and holding us.

We are too ready to believe the worst of other people and sometimes become jealous even of those who should be dearest to us. Forgive the mean promptings of our human nature and strengthen us to accept and support the divine calling of others, without desiring praise for ourselves.

V　God sent his Son into the world.
R　To bring us to eternal life.
V　Let us bless the Lord.
R　Thanks be to God.

✠

The shock, the sorrow, the surge of anger,
the desire to hurt the loved one who seemed
　　faithless –

did the black rage shake him when it was first
    made known?

But love prevailed, stronger than resentment;
there would be no scandal, no shaming, only a
    quiet ending
before the long years of loneliness after a hope
    that had failed.

Unquiet sleep, broken dreams,
came after a day of bitter decisions;
then a new vision, prompting, comforting,
    challenging –
something unheard, undreamed by any dreamer;
even Joseph of Egypt was never so highly
    favoured.

There was no turning back on the command of
    God,
though the calling baffled sense, defied language,
found no answer in the familiar, loved religion.

Only a love too faithful for consummation
could make ready for a holy birth.

In Nazareth gossips whispered, sniggered,
    pointed:
a dusty road lay open towards Bethlehem.

✠

*Grant me the trust of Joseph, last and greatest of
the patriarchs.*

*Grant me the humble love of Joseph, husband of
Mary.*

*Grant me the strong wisdom of Joseph, protector of
Jesus.*

# 6

# Birth of Jesus

V   We adore thee O Christ and we bless thee.
R   Because by thy wonderful Nativity thou hast
     given us new birth.

*In those days a decree went out from the Emperor
Augustus that all the world should be registered.
All went to their own towns to be registered. Joseph
also went from the town of Nazareth in Galilee to
Judaea, to the city of David called Bethlehem,
because he was descended from the house and
family of David. He went to be registered with
Mary, to whom he was engaged and who was
expecting a child. When they were there, the time
came for her to deliver her child. And she gave
birth to her firstborn son and wrapped him in
bands of cloth, and laid him in a manger, because
there was no place for them in the inn.*

(Luke 2: part of verses 1–7)

The time had come. The Messiah, so long
promised, was born at last. But he came in a way
none of the prophets had foretold, humbly and

unregarded. His divinity was concealed, but his humanity was laid in a loving mother's arms, guarded by a man chosen to act to him as a father. Redemption had come to the world, though the world did not yet know it.

We give thanks for the wonderful gift of God's own Son. As we pass our lives in a world that has been favoured by supreme love, we rejoice in our human nature restored to the image of God who made it. May we have grace to reflect on this great mystery and to adore the Child of Bethlehem who is the Light of the World.

We are too casual in our response to the wonder of the Nativity. We listen to the Christmas story and sing the Christmas hymns without deeply reverencing the amazing grace of which they tell. We are sentimental when we should be full of awe. Forgive the forgetfulness of familiarity, and give us more love for the One who took our human nature upon himself.

V   God sent his Son into the world.
R   To bring us to eternal life.
V   Let us bless the Lord.
R   Thanks be to God.

✠

It was the word of prophecy through the long
  years of waiting,
the word known only to a woman and a man in
  the few months of waiting,
the Word before all time, now new-begotten at a
  chosen time.

The past promise became present reality
in the harsh reality of an outhouse,
the breathing reality of animals,
the alien reality of an unfamiliar town,
the ignorant reality of those who slept in comfort.

Angels had promised great things, a birth by the
  Spirit,
a new life different from any life since the sun set
  on Eden.

But here was no place for prophet, priest or
  king:
bare walls, earth floor, feeding-trough for a bed.

They needed all their faith, Mary and Joseph,
to go on believing in the angelic visitations.

They wondered at the helplessness of the baby,
who was foretold as the Son of the Almighty.

Parent-like, they wanted so much for him:
peace and security instead of this rejection, this
     homeless state:
something better than the pressure of rough
     wood on gentle flesh.

✠

*Child of Bethlehem, weak and helpless, have pity
on my weakness.*

*Child of Bethlehem, loved and cherished, forgive
my lack of love.*

*Child of Bethlehem, peaceful in a manger, calm
my restlessness.*

*Great Son of God made flesh, hold me in your
strong arms.*

# Shepherds and Angels

V   We adore thee O Christ and we bless thee.
R   Because by thy wonderful Nativity thou hast given us new birth.

*In that region there were shepherds living in the fields, keeping watch over their flock by night. Then an angel of the Lord stood before them, and the glory of the Lord shone around them, and they were terrified. But the angel said to them, 'Do not be afraid, for see – I am bringing you good news of great joy for all the people: to you is born this day in the city of David a Saviour, who is the Messiah, the Lord. This will be a sign for you: you will find a child wrapped in bands of cloth and lying in a manger.' And suddenly there was with the angel a multitude of the heavenly host, praising God and saying, 'Glory to God in the highest heaven, and on earth peace among those whom he favours.'*
(Luke 2: 8–14)

The life of a shepherd was hard, spending much of the time outdoors in all weathers, constantly

watchful for predators and for sheep who wandered away from the flock. In the Bible the figure of the shepherd is often used as a type of those charged by God with the care of his people. More wonderfully, it is also applied to God's caring love, and Jesus spoke specifically of himself as the Good Shepherd. It was shepherds who had the privilege of first being told that the Messiah was born and that he would be the Saviour of the whole world.

**We praise God for the assurance that his mercy extends to all humanity; that Christ was born to save any who would accept his pardoning love. We give thanks for the many ways in which the good news has been made known to us and to the whole world, and for the signs of glory that are all around us if we will look with the eyes of faith.**

**We too often act as if true Christianity was only to be found in the church or group to which we belong. Even when we share fellowship with others, we keep a secret sense of our own superiority. Forgive our narrow minds, open our closed hearts to learn from different ways of expressing faith, and keep us always ready to hear the messages of divine love.**

V  God sent his Son into the world.
R  **To bring us to eternal life.**
V  Let us bless the Lord.
R  **Thanks be to God.**

An ordinary night, a peaceful night offering no
   disturbance
unless from the odd wolf, or the silly strayer
that might mean a long search in the darkness
when ninety-nine were behaving themselves.

They did not think they were particularly good
   shepherds –
just men with a job to do, flocks and families to
   keep,
quiet men, not highly regarded in the courts and
   cities.

The glory of the Lord was not something that
   concerned them:
the Rabbi might have mentioned it in forgotten
   schooldays
as appearing to Moses, Elijah and such great
   ones.

It was not for them, but it came upon them,
it shone, revealed, terrified,
and brought words of peace, comfort, favour –
little enough of them in the cold fields –
and of the Messiah all hoped for, few expected,
all because of a birth in a little place, not far off.

Somehow the glory, the promises, so far above
    them,
were really for them, startled night watchers,
because that child was lying in a manger
born among their own kind, the simple people
who would be around on an ordinary night.

✠

*Glory to God in the highest, hidden among the
    humble.*
*Glory to God in the highest, revealed to the poor
    and lowly.*
*Glory to God in the highest, come to the earth he
    created.*
*Great shepherd, be merciful to your silly,
    wandering sheep.*

GLORIA·IN·PROFUNDIS

# 8

# Shepherds at the Manger

V   We adore thee O Christ and we bless thee.
R   Because by thy glorious Nativity thou hast
given us new birth.

*When the angels had left them and gone into
heaven, the shepherds said to one another, 'Let us
go now to Bethlehem and see this thing which has
taken place, which the Lord has made known to
us.' So they went with haste and found Mary and
Joseph, and the child lying in the manger. When
they saw this, they made known what had been
told them about this child, and all who heard it
were amazed at what the shepherds told them. But
Mary treasured all these words and pondered them
in her heart. The shepherds returned, glorifying
and praising God for all they had heard and seen,
as it had been told them.*

(Luke 2: 15–20)

Faithful to the word of the angel, the shepherds
went to see for themselves what God had done.
The poverty and humility of the scene in the stable

did not disturb their faith. It was all as they had been told, and they rejoiced that the Saviour was born. They began at once to proclaim the good news. Mary responded quietly to the marvellous promise that had been fulfilled.

We give thanks for the divinity that is in all people because God has taken our nature upon him. We are comforted and joyful to know that he speaks not only to the wise and the mighty but to all who are open to receive his word and respond with faith.

Too often we fail to see the glory that is all around us and to find the presence of God in the simplest things of this world. We do not value the quiet goodness of people whose lives seem unremarkable. Help us to discern Christ everywhere and in all, and to rejoice in knowing his continual presence with us.

V   God sent his Son into the world.
R   To bring us to eternal life.
V   Let us bless the Lord.
R   Thanks be to God.

✠

It was no royal court, no place for a king to be
     born,
no hallowed sanctuary where a priest should
     enter,
no walled security for a vulnerable new baby.

Few would turn aside to see evidence of another
     birth,
another life in this land where promises seemed
     forgotten
and foreign rulers demanded their dues from the
     poor.

But it was a fair sight, something acceptable,
understood by those who lived close to animals;
it was what they had expected – no ceremony,
nothing to hold one simplicity apart from
     another.

It had been a good angel, a messenger of truth,
for the glory of the Word is in its fulfilment
not in the qualifications that we lay upon it.

They praised God in loud voices,
the voices of men who could call far across the
     hills,
and took on themselves the role of angels among
     their own kind.

But Mary was silent in the mystery of grace,
in the silence that can be the highest praise of
    God.

✠

*Give me, dear Christ Child, ears to hear the
    message of the angels.*
*Give me, dear Christ Child, lips to make known
    your love.*
*Give me, dear Christ Child, the wisdom of silent
    adoration.*

# 9

# Circumcision or Naming of Jesus

V   We adore thee O Christ and we bless thee.

R   **Because by thy wonderful Nativity thou hast given us new birth.**

*After eight days had passed, it was time to circumcise the child; and he was called Jesus, the name given by the angel before he was conceived in the womb.*                (Luke 2: 15–20)

The earthly life of Jesus begins with an act of obedience, as he himself would be obedient to his heavenly Father even to the end. Following the Jewish Law for male children, he was circumcised and named a week after his birth. The name commanded by the angel of the Annunciation is given public declaration. He is Jesus, 'Jehovah saves', and the salvation will be for all people.

**We praise the holy name of Jesus above all names. We give thanks that the Saviour of the world was**

born as man, giving us a pattern of obedience for
our religious duties, to be the outward sign of our
inward love and faith. We give thanks that we are
given grace and commandment to pray to the
Father in his name.

If we trust to ourselves, we can easily go astray
in our religion. Sometimes we raise the perfor-
mance of public worship above the need for
private prayer and for lives that follow the divine
will. At other times we are slack and think that if
we pray alone we do not need to join in prayer
with other Christians. Help us to honour the name
of Jesus both in our hearts and in the fellowship of
the Church.

V   God sent his Son into the world.
R   To bring us to eternal life.
V   Let us bless the Lord.
R   Thanks be to God.

✠

Names are the signals which make people real to
    us,
names we love are the dearest sounds of our
    lives.

Names can be a screen, concealing a person
    behind a word.

One Name only links God and our humanity
and makes us bold to give expression to the
    inexpressible.

The Name of Jesus brings the faithful to their
    knees;
but to the unbelieving it is a dead echo of things
    past,
and to the angry and impatient becomes an
    obscenity.

But for Mary and Joseph, the Name meant a little
    baby
to be loved and protected and made obedient to
    the Law.

It is the holy Name that calls the child made new
    by water,
the hope of the old who utter it as breath comes
    slowly,
and mercy to those who use it in vain,
for he loves them too and will love them to the
    end.

✠

*At the name of Jesus*
> *every knee should bend*
> *in heaven and on earth and under the earth,*
*and every tongue should confess*
*that Jesus Christ is Lord*
> *to the glory of God the Father.*

*May I honour that dear Name more truly, on my lips and in my heart.*

# 10

# Magi

V   We adore thee O Christ and we bless thee.
R   Because by thy wonderful Nativity thou hast
    given us new birth.

*In the time of King Herod, after Jesus was born in
Bethlehem of Judaea, wise men from the east came
to Jerusalem, asking, 'Where is the child who has
been born king of the Jews? For we have observed
his star at its rising, and have come to do him
homage.' When King Herod heard this, he was
frightened, and all Jerusalem with him; and calling together all the chief priests and scribes of the
people, he inquired of them where the Messiah was
to be born. They told him, 'In Bethlehem of
Judaea.' Then he sent them to Bethlehem saying,
'Go and search diligently for the child; and when
you have found him, bring me word so that I may
also go and pay him homage.' When they had
heard the king, they set out; and there, ahead of
them, went the star that they had seen at its rising,
until it stopped over the place where the child was.
On entering the house, they saw the child with*

*Mary his mother; and they knelt down and paid
him homage. Then, opening their treasure-chests,
they offered him gifts of gold, frankincense and
myrrh.* (Matthew 2: part of verses 1–12)

The 'wise men' have been subject to more legendary additions than any other part of the Nativity
story. They have been given names and described
as kings, but the Greek word in the gospel is
*magi*, which was widely used of those who prac-
tised magic and divination. These men may have
come from anywhere in the Middle East region:
the point of the story is that they were the first
Gentiles to visit and worship the Christ Child,
offering him gifts which relate to his kingship,
priesthood and sacrificial death.

**We give thanks that the Incarnation was for all
people; that God makes a new covenant with any
who will come to him in faith. We ask for grace to
offer our gifts of love and obedience. They are all
that we can give him, but he graciously accepts
them if they are offered in the name of Jesus. May
we be watchful for his many ways of guiding us,
and joyful to follow them.**

**Although we have learned and experienced so
much of the steadfast love of God, we are still
hesitant in following where he leads, as the Magi
followed his guiding star. We do not make our-**

selves open to his calling, and we are grudging in our response. Help us to seek diligently after his will and to make our lives richer in worship.

V   God sent his Son into the world.
**R   To bring us to eternal life.**
V   Let us bless the Lord.
**R   Thanks be to God.**

Gold for a king, for the King of the Jews,
and King of all the earth, for he made it:
stoop under the low lintel of humility,
to fall before him throned in a cradle.

Incense for a priest, for the High Priest of the
    Covenant,
rising over the sacrifices that unite divine and
    human:
these rough walls contain the Holy of Holies,
where all may enter into a greater Covenant.

Myrrh for the dead, for those whose life returns
    to the Giver,
yielding the breath that was granted for a span of
    years:
learn from this Child that the cradle leads to the
    tomb,
but the anointed body is not the end of the story.

Mary and Joseph wonder at the strange visitors
who are brought to their knees before their loved
   fragility;
not yet knowing of the royal title
to be nailed over the priestly sacrifice, silent in
   death.

*Star of Bethlehem, guide me onward*

   *to the banquet of the King*

   *to the pardoning by the Priest*

   *to the life beyond death.*

# 11

## Presentation

V   We adore thee O Christ and we bless thee.
R   Because by thy glorious Nativity thou hast given us new birth.

*When the time came for their purification according to the law of Moses, they brought him up to Jerusalem to present him to the Lord. Now there was a man in Jerusalem whose name was Simeon. It had been revealed to him by the Holy Spirit that he would not see death before he had seen the Lord's Messiah. Guided by the Spirit, Simeon came into the Temple; and when the parents brought in the child Jesus, to do for him what was customary under the law, Simeon took him in his arms and praised God, saying,*

*'Master, now you are dismissing your servant in*
  *peace,*
    *according to your word;*
*for my eyes have seen your salvation,*
*which you have prepared in the presence of all*
  *peoples,*
    *a light for revelation to the Gentiles*
    *and for glory to your people Israel.'*

*Then Simeon blessed them and said to his mother
Mary, 'A sword will pierce your own soul too.'*

(Luke 2: part of verses 22–35)

Forty days after the birth of Jesus, Mary and
Joseph went to make their offering as the Law
commanded (Leviticus 12: 6–8). This religious
duty brought a further revelation that Jesus the
Messiah was born for the salvation of the whole
human race. Simeon, a devout worshipper after
the Old Covenant, was given a vision of what
would come to pass under the New.

**We give thanks for the gift of light by which we
receive the word of God and can see the tokens of
his presence all around us. We praise the salvation
brought by this Holy Child and pray that the light
of his grace will shine within us and through us,
keeping us faithful to the end when we may depart
in peace.**

**We too often observe our religious duties in a
casual way, and sometimes resent the time that
they require, failing to accept the peace that they
can bring. Help us to come with joy to our worship, resolved to open our hearts to what God is
showing us, so that we may receive and declare the
word of revelation.**

V    God sent his Son into the world.
**R    To bring us to eternal life.**
V    Let us bless the Lord.
**R    Thanks be to God.**

God said, Let there be light,
and for ever after there was light for those who
    would see it,
and no darkness of sin or sorrow could quench
    the light.

Light reveals the visible signs of God's glory
and the secret signs of his grace:
for light itself is his glory, awesome,
    unapproachable,
and also the grace that is intimate, inviting all to
    the Child.

Light reveals the true state of our being,
the hidden things that we would rather not have
    known,
penetrates like a scalpel the festering wounds of
    sin.

If a sword would pierce the most pure heart of
    Mary,
none can escape the sword of judgement at the
    last –
except by the love in the eyes of the Child
that lets us depart in peace.

Because he is the Word of salvation who reads us
in the light of mercy.

*That was the true Light, coming into the world.*

*Lord, give me light to know my sinfulness*

    *give me light to see your salvation*

    *give me light to overcome the darkness of
death.*

# 12

# Flight into Egypt

V  We adore thee O Christ and we bless thee.
R  **Because by thy wonderful Nativity thou hast given us new birth.**

*An angel of the Lord appeared to Joseph in a dream and said, 'Get up, take the child and his mother and flee to Egypt, and remain there until I tell you; for Herod is about to search for the child, to destroy him.' Then Joseph got up, took the child and his mother by night, and went to Egypt, and remained there until the death of Herod.*

(Matthew 2: 13–15)

While shepherds and Magi adored the Child, Joseph had been in the background, quietly watching and caring for his wife: now he was urgently called to action to protect the Son of God. Escaping the jealous rage of Herod, they fled southward to Egypt, the land from which their ancestors had been brought out of slavery.

**We give thanks for all who protect the weak and**

vulnerable and pray that they may be given strength to fulfil their calling; and for the divine love that uses our frailty to support one another in need. We pray for guidance in all times of danger and uncertainty.

We do not open ourselves fully to God's ways of guiding; we stand aside while others act to help those in need. Make us more ready to care not only for those near to us but for the stranger and the outcast, the homeless and those who flee from persecution.

V   God sent his Son into the world.
R   To bring us to eternal life.
V   Let us bless the Lord.
R   Thanks be to God.

✠

God's protecting darkness concealed their flight
from the dark jealousy that feared the
      defenceless.

They had to leave the Promised Land,
go back through the wilderness to the place of
      slavery.

God who had carried his people in the
    wandering years
made the return journey in a mother's arms,
divine power diminished into a bundle of
    humanity.

They were not the first to flee from tyranny
or the last to stumble across a strange frontier,
to seek safety among alien faces
when the familiar took on a face of doom.

In time the Child would welcome the stranger,
the outcast, the despised, the unprotected,
with a royal love that kings dared not feel
because the ground beneath the throne might be
    shaken.

✠

*On wanderers without a home: Lord have mercy.*

*On refugees driven by war and violence: Lord
have mercy.*

*On my hardness of heart when help is needed:
Lord have mercy.*

# 13

# Massacre of the Innocents

V   We adore thee O Christ and we bless thee.

R   Because by thy wonderful Nativity thou hast
given us new birth.

*When Herod saw that he had been tricked by the
wise men, he was infuriated, and he sent and
killed all the children in and around Bethlehem
who were two years old or under, according to the
time that he had learned from the wise men. Then
was fulfilled what had been spoken through the
prophet Jeremiah:*

*A voice was heard in Ramah,*
*wailing and loud lamentation.*
*Rachel weeping for her children;*
*she refused to be comforted,*
*because they are no more.*

(Matthew 2: 16–18)

Like all tyrants, Herod feared any challenge to his
position. No star would guide him to the real King
of the Jews and he thought he had made himself

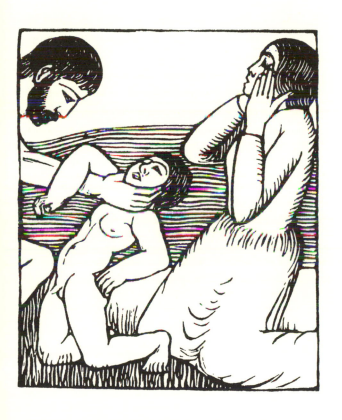

secure when he murdered all the infants in the region of Bethlehem. He did not know that the one he sought was safely away from his power, and that he himself had not long to live. The wonderful birth of Jesus brought a cruel response from an evil heart, as many today still refuse his offered love.

**We give thanks for the faith that grants us light in darkness, to see divine love at work even through suffering. Help us to hold fast when hope fails and understanding is dimmed, ever to trust in Christ who brings new life out of death.**

**We close our eyes to the suffering that does not come near us; we too readily ignore the abuse of power that does not touch us. Give us strength to speak for those whose voices are not heard, and to reach out in love to those whose hearts are broken.**

V   God sent his Son into the world.
R   To bring us to eternal life.
V   Let us bless the Lord.
R   Thanks be to God.

Death came with a new face into the village,
not with the familiar sword of sickness
or striking through the perils that evade a
    mother's care.

The royal swords, forged for confrontation of
  equals,
flashed like deadly lightning in a clear day;
mothers cried out to an empty sky where no
  angels descended,
demanding to know why God had forsaken
  them.

It was not the first or the last time
that innocence would be harried into death:
and the pain would never be lessened by sharing
or the mystery of suffering be made clear.

One mother was spared to hold her child in
  safety
until the time of agony by the soul-piercing
  sword.

One child lived, to grow into perfect manhood,
suffer a greater torment, break the tyranny of
  death.

✠

*Lord, take our hearts of stone and give us hearts
  of flesh:*

*restore lost innocence, that we may relieve the
  innocent.*

# 14

# Return to Nazareth

V  We adore thee O Christ and we bless thee.
R  Because by thy wonderful Nativity thou hast given us new birth.

*When Herod died, an angel of the Lord suddenly appeared to Joseph in Egypt and said, 'Get up, take the child and his mother, and go into the land of Israel, for those who were seeking the child's life are dead.' Then Joseph got up, took the child and his mother, and went to the land of Israel. But when he heard that Archelaus was ruling over Judaea in place of his father Herod, he was afraid to go there. And after being warned in a dream, he went away to the district of Galilee. There he made his home in a town called Nazareth.*

(Matthew 2: 19–23)

After the joys and perils of the birth of Jesus, the Holy Family moved quietly back to Nazareth where the first announcement of God's purpose had been made. Jesus began the years of growing and learning, and the life of a family home, until

the time should come for his ministry to begin.

**We give thanks for our homes, for the shared joy of families and the quiet happiness of daily life. Grant that the pattern of our lives may be governed by the grace that was in the home at Nazareth, as Jesus grew from infancy to manhood.**

We do not always value as we should the simple blessings of life. We would like each day to bring a special pleasure or a new personal success. Give us contentment in the day and the hour of opportunity, with grateful hearts for our creation and preservation.

V   God sent his Son into the world.
R   To bring us to eternal life.
V   Let us bless the Lord.
R   Thanks be to God.

✠

The time of waiting was not yet over.

Centuries of expectation had ended with a host of
   angels,
with great wonder among the simple and the
   wise,
and flight from the shedding of innocent blood.

The final time appointed would not come
until God had lived the full experience:
learned to walk, read, reason, labour for a living,
and the Maker came to the maturity of his human
   image.

Before the battle with evil was begun,
life was blessed in the little things,
and there was grace in a humble house;
and light would for ever shine in darkness
because God had visited and redeemed his
   people.

*Jesus bearer of our humanity,*

*Mary gracious, gentle Mother,*

*Joseph faithful, loving protector,*

   *have mercy on us.*

*May God grant that the Holy Family of Nazareth
shall be our protection and guide day by day and
year by year, leading us to the full revelation of
glory.*

# After the Stations

*Almighty God, grant to us, who have followed our Lord through the time of his coming to earth, the peace promised by the angels, the simple trust of the shepherds, the wise discernment of the Magi, and the love of the Holy Family in our homes and in all our lives, through Jesus Christ our Saviour.*

A hymn may be sung; see p. 1.

A priest who is present may give this blessing, or the people may say it together, saying 'us' for 'you':

*May God give you grace to follow the example of Christ, and bring you through the power of his Incarnation to eternal life, and the blessing of God Almighty, the Father, the Son and the Holy Spirit, be among you and remain with you always. Amen.*

# A Little Anthology of the Nativity

Since fear and pain were not excluded,
grace descending gave them no cover;
to be homeless at such a time was a misfortune
rich in precedent, plentifully followed.

In that ordinary moment it was accomplished;
the decision to register new flesh
remained open, unprejudiced by time,
covenanted permission for survival.

In that unchartered moment God was born,
thirsted, died, rose, returned in flame;
a rabble ran free from the desert
through undivided waters of the womb.

In that aching moment the sand was red,
Augustine walked in the orchard, Aquinas prayed,
the centuries joined hands, broke bread together,
issued subtle heresies, compendious denials.

The dove-stricken eagle staggered,
and cried in pain for old gods dead.
Bethlehemites were otherwise engaged;
Herod slept in scarlet while shepherds watched.

*R.C.*

The reason of this coming down was because of
us, and our transgression called forth the loving-
kindness of the Word, that the Lord should both
make haste to help us and appear among men.
For of his becoming incarnate we were the object,
and for our salvation he dealt so lovingly as to
appear and be born even in a human body.

*St Athanasius*

O the magnitude of meekness!
    Worth from worth immortal sprung;
O the strength of infant weakness,
    If eternal is so young!

*Christopher Smart*

Man was made in God's image. The significance of
this truth is that in that original constitution of
mankind lies, as the Fathers saw, the prophecy of
the divine Incarnation and the grounds of its
possibility. God can express himself in his own

image, he can express himself therefore in manhood, he can show himself as man. And conversely, in the occurrence of the Incarnation lies the supreme evidence of the real moral likeness of man to God.

*Charles Gore*

Think on th' eternal home
    The Saviour left for you;
Think on the Lord most holy, come
    To dwell with hearts untrue:
So shall ye tread untired his pastoral ways,
And in the darkness sing your carol of high
    praise.

*John Keble*

He who gave the Son of God a body for time can give us a body for eternity. he called him out of eternity to live in time and gave him a body. He calls us out of time into eternity, and gives to us, the sons of God, an immortal body. All our faith is grounded upon the Incarnation of the Son of God.

*A. H. Stanton*

I saw a stable, low and very bare,
      A little child in a manger.
The oxen knew him, had him in their care,
      To men he was a stranger.
The safety of the world was lying there,
      And the world's danger.

*Mary Coleridge*

Welcome, all wonders in one sight!
      Eternity shut in a span!
Summer in winter! Day in night!
      Heaven in earth! and God in Man!
Great Little One, whose all-embracing birth,
Lifts earth to heaven, stoops heaven to earth.

*Richard Crashaw*

I think that the purpose and cause of the Incarnation was that God might illuminate the world by his wisdom and excite it to the love of himself.

*Peter Abelard*

Moonless darkness stands between.
Past, O Past, no more be seen!
But the Bethlehem star may lead me
To the sight of him who freed me
From the self that I have been.
Make me pure, Lord: thou art holy;
Make me meek, Lord: thou wert lowly;
Now beginning, and alway:
Now begin, on Christmas day.

*Gerard Manley Hopkins*

Christ is both David's Son and David's Lord: David's Lord always, David's Son in time: David's Lord, born of the substance of his Father, David's Son, born of the Virgin Mary, conceived by the Holy Ghost. Let us hold fast both. The one of them will be our eternal habitation. The other is our deliverance from our present exile. For unless our Lord Jesus Christ had vouchsafed to become man, man had perished. He was made that which he

made, that what he made might not perish. Very
Man, Very God; God and man, whole Christ. This
is the Catholic faith.

*St Augustine*

Praise to the Holiest in the height,
And in the depth be praise,
In all his works most wonderful,
Most sure in all his ways.

O loving wisdom of our God!
When all was sin and shame,
A second Adam to the fight
And to the rescue came.

O wisest love! that flesh and blood,
Which did in Adam fail,
Should strive afresh against the foe,
Should strive and should prevail.

And that a higher gift than grace
Should flesh and blood refine,
God's presence and his very self,
And essence all divine.

*J. H. Newman*

# A Note on the Illustrations
# by Winefride Pruden

*Cover   The Presentation in the Temple.* A cloisonné enamel icon of the late twelfth century from Georgia. Metalwork, including enamels, could be described as the national art of Georgia, which also developed a local style of architecture (seen in the background) that was not strictly Byzantine. The artist has shown Simeon as the old man that St Luke's Gospel indicates, but the prophetess Anna seems to wear her eighty-four years very lightly. St Joseph too, eagerly thrusting forward his offering of two turtle doves, looks in the prime of life; and indeed, we know nothing authentic to the contrary.
Photograph by Edgar Holloway.

*Frontispiece   Madonna and Child.* A wood-engraving of 1923 by Eric Gill. Many of these were not used for printing, but were cut out of their blocks and exhibited to be sold as ornamental plaques.
Copyright © the estate of Eric Gill

*Before the Stations* Bambino. A wood-engraving of 1927 by Eric Gill, one of the illustrations for *Gloria in Profundis*, a book of poems by G. K. Chesterton. The type of swaddled infant is derived from Early Christian art, and a variant had been used by Gill for a Christmas card in 1920.
Copyright as above.

*Chapter 1 The Annunciation to Zechariah.* This manuscript illustration is from an Ethiopian Book of the Gospels in the British Library. Few early Ethiopian manuscripts survived the Muslim destructions of the sixteenth century. They were influenced by Byzantium, and have some affinities with Romanesque art. From the sixteenth and seventeenth centuries, Portuguese and other European explorers and missionaries introduced more naturalistic styles, but Ethiopians always resisted the use of perspective. This artist is unashamedly anachronistic, placing crosses in the hands of both Zechariah and the angel, and representing the temple as a Christian church.
By courtesy of the British Library.

*Chapter 2 The Annunciation.* This is an unusual interpretation of the subject by a North Italian painter, Lorenzo Lotto (1480–1556), in the church of Reconati near Loreto. Lotto seems to have been a difficult and possibly disturbed person, who

eventually became a lay brother in the monastery
of the Santa Casa in nearby Loreto. His troubled
mind is reflected in this picture, in which the cat
appears terrified by the angel. God the Father
appears in the clouds, sending down the Holy
Spirit.

*Chapter 3   The Visitation.* A twelfth-century wall-
painting from the convent of Sigena in Northern
Spain, fortunately photographed before the build-
ing was destroyed in the Spanish Civil War.
Obviously, realism was not the artist's major concern. The two expectant mothers show no signs of
their pregnancy, and Elizabeth looks as young as
Mary, who can be identified by the star on her
maphorian. The influence of mosaics in Norman
Sicily is seen in the Byzantine head-dresses, but
the faces are more classical. The scrolls, from
which the lettering has flaked off, would once
have borne their salutations: in Elizabeth's case
*Benedicta tu inter muliere,* and in Mary's
*Magnificat anima mea Dominum.*

*Chapter 4   The Birth of John the Baptist.* A painting by the Sienese artist Giovanni di Paolo (1403–
82/3) in the National Gallery, London. This subject
was less popular than *The Birth of the Virgin,* in
medieval art, though the two scenes were almost
indistinguishable unless the sex of the child was

visible or unless, as in this case, the figure of Zechariah writing was included. Both took place in well-furnished houses, very different from the stable at Bethlehem. Usually, homely touches are included, such as this midwife airing a towel before the fire.

By courtesy of the National Gallery, London.

*Chapter 5    Joseph's Dream.* Part of a twelfth century mural from the convent of Sigena in Northern Spain, sadly destroyed in the Spanish Civil War. These paintings are of particular interest in England because they have a close resemblance to the illustrations in the Winchester Bible. In early times, artists and craftsmen, recommended by one court, abbey or cathedral chapter to another, travelled much more widely than is realized by the average package tourist today. In Early Christian and medieval art, Joseph only appears as an accessory figure in scenes of the lives of Christ and the Virgin. At the Counter-Reformation, promoted by St Teresa of Avila and St Ignatius Loyola, Joseph acquired a cult as a saint in his own right. In early art, he nearly always wears a worried expression, racked by doubts about Mary's virtue, or by his responsibilities as protector of the Holy Child. The usual arrangement of the hair coiled round the ear suggests a connection with the mosaics in Norman Sicily, where this coiffure is also found.

*Chapter 6    The Nativity*. This wood-engraving by David Jones (1895–1974) is an illustration for his *Child's Rosary Book*. At the time, he was still a novice in wood-engraving, but the rather clumsy execution makes the scene more, rather than less, effective in its combined tenderness and reverence. Later, after much practice and study in preparation for illustrating the *Chester Play of the Deluge*, he achieved greater fluency.

Copyright David Jones Trustees.

*Chapter 7    Shepherds and Angels*. This wood-engraving was cut by Eric Gill in 1923, after a drawing (originally coloured by hand) by his eldest daughter Elizabeth. He always encouraged his children to provide illustrations for Christmas cards and for *The Game*, the occasional magazine which he helped to produce.

Copyright © the estate of Eric Gill

*Chapter 8    Shepherds at the Manger*. This wood-engraving by Eric Gill was one of the illustrations for *Gloria in Profundis*, a book of poems by G. K. Chesterton, published in 1927.

Copyright © the estate of Eric Gill

*Chapter 9    The Circumcision*. A painting by Giovanni Bellini (c. 1400–1516) in the National Gallery, London. In the medieval church, this

event was seen as significant because it was the
first occasion on which the Redeemer's blood was
shed; but the exclusively Jewish nature of the rite
made it unattractive to Christians. At the Counter-
Reformation, however, the Jesuits, with their devotion to the Holy Name of Jesus, emphasized the
fact that the Circumcision was also a naming
ceremony, and representations of it became more
popular.

*Chapter 10    The Magi.* A sixth-century mosaic in
Sant' Apollinare, Ravenna. The Magi were one of
the earliest subjects in Christian art. They were
seen as the first Gentiles who recognized the
Messiah whom the Jews rejected. They had
already been represented on the walls of the cata-
combs where, as here in Ravenna, they conformed
to St Matthew's description of 'wise men from the
East', probably Persian astrologers. Later artists
indulged their fancy by dressing them in royal
robes, following Tertullian's identification of them
with Old Testament prophecies of kings bringing
gifts. It was at Ravenna that they were first labelled
with names, discovered in an apocryphal Gospel.
They were regarded as symbolic of the three con-
tinents then known, and of the Three Ages of
Man. It was only when the vastness of Africa was
revealed by explorers that Balthasar was invested
with a black skin.

*The Sleep of the Magi.* This twelfth-century carv-
ing by Gislebert from the cathedral of Autun is an
example of several scenes representing these char-
acters who were among the most popular in
Christian art. The Adoration of the Magi is familiar
to everyone, but there were also pictures of the
Journey of the Magi, which was an excuse for
artists to paint exotic attendants, splendidly capari-
soned horses or camels, monkeys and leopards.
They are often seen, as here, being warned by the
angel not to return to Herod. They always share
a bed, wearing their crowns or other fantastic
headgear.
Photograph by Edgar Holloway.

*Chapter 11   The Presentation.* This is another
example of Georgian metalwork as seen in the
cover picture, but in this case, instead of an
enamel it is a silver plaque of the eleventh century, striking in its simplicity and monumentality.
Photograph by Edgar Holloway.

*Chapter 12   The Flight into Egypt.* A carved stone
capital from the cathedral of Autun in Burgundy,
c.1130. The sculptor Gislebert or Giselbertus is
one of the few Romanesque artists whose identity
we know, as he signed his name over the portal
of the cathedral. This subject was very popular,
with variants such as *The Rest on the Flight into*

*Egypt*, or scenes of legendary miracles occurring on the way.

*Chapter 13    The Slaughter of the Innocents.* A wood-engraving by Eric Gill for the cover of a catalogue for an exhibition held in Burgess Hill in 1914, in aid of Belgian refugees. It was originally intended for a Gospel Book planned the previous year, but the idea was abandoned because Gill, according to his Diary, 'came to the conclusion that project too big for me to undertake'. In later years, of course, such a project was to be one of his greatest achievements. Most artists who have represented this subject have shown it as a crowd scene full of violent incident; but Gill's more economical interpretation loses none of the emotional impact.

Copyright © the estate of Eric Gill

*Chapter 14    The Return to Galilee.* Although the Flight into Egypt was one of the most popular subjects, the return seems to have been regarded by artists as something of an anticlimax. This rare example is from a fourteenth-century Italian manuscript of a *Meditation on the Life of Christ* by the Pseudo-Bonaventura. Christ is, of course, no longer an infant, and the fact that he is riding on the ass may have been intended as prophetic of his Entry into Jerusalem.

By courtesy of the President and Fellows of Corpus Christi College, Oxford.

*Anthology   Madonna and Child, 1924.* This is another of Eric Gill's efforts to encourage his daughters' interest in art. In this case he has made a copper engraving after a drawing by his youngest daughter Joanna.

Copyright © the estate of Eric Gill